TRAIL OF TEARS

A History from Beginning to End

Copyright © 2019 by Hourly History.

All rights reserved.

Table of Contents

Introduction
Background
Settlers Move West
Andrew Jackson and the Indian Removal Act
Choctaw Removal in 1831
Seminole Removal in 1832
Creek Removal in 1834
Chickasaw Removal in 1837
Cherokee Removal in 1838
Legacy
Conclusion

Introduction

In the decade following the passage of the Indian Removal Act by the United States Congress in 1830, the U.S. administration began a policy of forced relocation under which many thousands of Native American people were removed from their traditional homelands and sent to areas with which they had no historical connection and which forced them to change their way of life. Some of these relocations were undertaken with extreme brutality and led directly to the deaths of thousands of people. Those who survived the relocations found themselves living in unfamiliar areas and sometimes amidst other hostile tribes.

These events have become generally known as the Trail of Tears, though that term originally applied only to the forced relocation of the Cherokee Nation in 1838. The events which formed the Trail of Tears did not end the Indian Wars or even the forced relocation of Native Americans, and these would continue until the end of the nineteenth century and beyond, but they did set the tone for the official attitude of the U.S. administration towards Native American people for the next hundred years.

This is a troubling episode in American history and one that is often glossed over in the romanticizing of the Old West. Native American people were treated appallingly and their suffering and death was seen as irrelevant when set against the spread of white settlement and culture. This book tells the fascinating, horrifying, and moving story of the Trail of Tears.

Chapter One

Background

"The ground on which we stand is sacred ground. It is the blood of our ancestors."

—Crow Chief

Even today, it is sometimes said that America was discovered in 1492 by Christopher Columbus. The truth is that by 1492 America had been the home to a number of culturally rich and diverse human societies with their own cultures, religions, and complex societies for more than 12,000 years.

The people who became Native Americans began to arrive in North America around 16,000 BCE. They came from Siberia, across a land bridge which existed at that time linking Asia with America. Then, around 11,000 BCE, sea levels rose, the land bridge was submerged, and the people who had come to America were cut off from the rest of the world. In other parts of the world, there was communication between different cultures and societies, and this contributed towards the exchange of ideas and the rapid development of new technologies and sciences as nomadic tribes of hunter-gatherers gradually developed into large groups of people living in sophisticated cities.

The relative isolation of North America precluded this kind of exchange of ideas. The tribes that emerged there had contact with other similar tribes, but not with radically different cultures. They developed complex religious beliefs, which often involved living in harmony with the natural world, but their use and grasp of technology barely advanced beyond the Stone Age.

When European settlers began to arrive in the early 1500s, they brought with them new sciences and technologies, which enabled the use of huge ships, horses, and modern weapons and armor. Against these, the Native American people were largely helpless, and for the next 300 years, the white settlers inexorably pushed the Native American people back from the east coast of America.

By the time of the American War of Independence in 1775, European settlers who had originated from Britain, France, and the Netherlands dominated the east coast of North America. The war centered around the 13 colonies' battle to escape British control. Not for the first time, Native American people were forced to choose sides. Many chose to fight for the British, mainly because they were afraid that independence would see further encroachment into their lands by settlers. Of course, Britain lost the war, America became independent, and the Native Americans who had chosen to fight for the British were proven right.

The Treaty of Paris, signed in 1783, brought the War of Independence to an end. However, the treaty made no mention of the Native American people, and it included clauses whereby the British handed the new United States of America all territory east of the Mississippi, south of the Great Lakes, and in the north of Florida. Both signatories to the treaty chose to ignore the fact that the British government had already signed treaties with several Native American tribes promising some of this land to them. When it came to balancing the rights of Native Americans against the need for more land for settlers, both British and Americans found the choice easy to make—agreements with "savages" could hardly be considered binding, after all.

The War of Independence left behind a legacy of distrust and enmity between the victorious colonists, who generally seemed to regard Native American people as merciless savages who had sided with a tyrannical and oppressive government, and Native Americans who developed an abiding distrust for white settlers and came to regard "solemn and binding" treaties as worthless.

In the 1780s and 1790s, there were a series of conflicts between American settlers and Native Americans. In part, these were fomented and encouraged by the British who maintained forts in Canada and in what were then known as Ohio Country and Illinois Country despite the fact that these areas had been ceded to the United States in the Treaty of Paris. The British clearly hoped that continuing attacks by Native Americans would help to destabilize the new U.S. government, and during the 1790s, around 1,500 U.S. settlers in Kentucky living close to the Ohio River were killed by Native Americans.

In 1790, President George Washington sent a large force of U.S. militia to mount an offensive against the Shawnee people in Indiana. The American troops were soundly defeated. In 1791, a much larger force of more than 2,000 militia troops was sent on a new campaign in Ohio to attack Native American warriors. This force was attacked by over 2,000 Shawnee and Miami warriors, and over 600 U.S. militia were killed before the remainder fled.

These early conflicts had two direct results. Firstly, the president authorized the formation of the Legion of the United States, a professional standing army. Up to this time, the defense of the U.S. had been undertaken exclusively by militias, but in the large-scale pitched battles of the early 1790s these had proved ineffective, and thus the first professional American army was created. The second thing that these conflicts created was a feeling amongst many Americans that Native American people were the enemy. Not only had they sided with the British during the War of Independence, but many of the tribes continued to act against U.S. interests in the years that followed. It was very clear that a large-scale conflict was brewing between white American settlers and the Native American tribes.

Chapter Two

Settlers Move West

"Go West, young man."

—Horace Greeley

Early American settlers quickly occupied all available lands to the east of the Appalachian Mountains. As new waves of immigrants continued to arrive in the New World, mainly from Europe, there was nowhere for them to go except to the west, into lands occupied by Native American people.

Many of the Native American tribes on the boundary of this expansion were extremely concerned, but individual tribes could do little in the face of increasing numbers of settlers. These Native American people were also suffering in several ways from contact with white settlers. New diseases decimated many tribespeople when the settlers first appeared. Native American people had no resistance to diseases such as smallpox, cholera, and diphtheria and even to lesser diseases such as influenza, chickenpox, and measles. Epidemics caused large-scale loss of life amongst many Native American tribes from the first arrival of white settlers. Smallpox, in particular, affected many tribes, and it returned in waves of illness that killed up to 90% of the native population.

Alcohol was another problem for the Native American people. White settlers brought with them distilled alcohol in the form of rum and other liquors. Distilleries and breweries were often amongst the first large buildings to be established in any new colony. Rum and brandy became popular items to be traded to Native American people who had no previous experience of distilled alcoholic beverages. The outcome was chronic alcoholism in tribes that had regular contact with white settlers, and this, in turn, led to poverty and the breakdown of Native American social orders.

In some cases, white settlers seem to have used alcohol deliberately to make Native American people less warlike. A chief of the Shawnee people told a missionary in 1773: "They come and bring rum into our towns, offer it to the Indians and say, drink; this they will do until they become quite beside themselves and act as though they were out of their heads."

It was amongst the Shawnee people that a new leader arose in the early 1800s who attempted to unite Native American people to fight against the settlement of lands by the seemingly inexhaustible waves of new settlers. Tenskwatawa ("the Prophet") urged all his followers to reject the ways of the white men and in particular to avoid the consumption of alcohol. Tenskwatawa claimed to have experienced a number of visions which told him that, if his followers returned to a more traditional way of life, they would be able to resist the expansion of white settlers.

The message that Tenskwatawa was offering found resonance with many Native American tribes, and he quickly became an important religious and political leader. In 1808, Tenskwatawa and his older brother Tecumseh set up a community near the confluence of the Tippecanoe and Wabash Rivers in present-day Indiana. This large community, which became known as Prophetstown, attracted disaffected Native Americans from a number of tribes and soon grew to be the largest Native American community in the Great Lakes region. Tecumseh emerged as the leader of a confederation of several thousand warriors from a range of tribes, the largest single confederation of Native American people.

Finally, the governor of Indiana Territory, William Henry Harrison, became sufficiently concerned that he raised a militia of around 1,000 men and in November 1811 marched them to a site close to the Tippecanoe River. He opened a dialogue with the Native American camp but, early on the morning of November 7, a large body of Native American warriors under the command of Tenskwatawa (Tecumseh was absent from Prophetstown at the time) attacked the U.S. militia camp. After a battle lasting for several hours, Harrison's forces were victorious and occupied and destroyed Prophetstown.

This meant the effective end of the Native American confederation led by Tecumseh and Tenskwatawa, but it left a legacy of distrust about both the aims of Native American tribes, who many Americans believed were supported and encouraged by the British. This seemed to be confirmed when, in 1812, Great Britain and the United States once again found themselves at war and a large number of Native American warriors under the leadership of Tecumseh fought on the side of the British. Part of the war aims of the British was to create a Native American state west of the Appalachian Mountains, which would block any further move to the west by American settlers and which would also therefore block any further extension of the territory controlled by the United States.

The war dragged on with little concrete result for either side until it was ended by the Treaty of Ghent in 1814. The British had asked for the creation of a Native American buffer state in the Northwest Territory. This was refused by the American negotiators, but the final treaty did include a clause at the insistence of the British which affirmed that Native American tribes would be assured of "all possessions, rights and privileges which they may have enjoyed, or been entitled to in 1811."

In theory, this meant that U.S. settlers could not move into areas that had been possessions of Native American people before 1811. Unsurprisingly, this clause of the Treaty of Ghent had little effect on the rate or scale of U.S. expansion into territory in the west. It was also notable that no representatives of Native American tribes were involved in the negotiations or consulted about what was agreed upon. They were simply told after the event what had been negotiated by Great Britain and the United States.

The War of 1812 reinforced the feeling amongst Americans that Native Americans were the enemy, siding once again with America's most bitter enemy and attempting to block the expansion of the United States to the west. For Native American people, this war and the treaty that followed simply confirmed that white people and their treaties were not to be trusted and that the fine words used in such treaties did not necessarily translate into appropriate action.

The position seemed intractable. On one side, the United States wanted to push its frontiers as far west as possible and planned to do this by an influx of settlers. Native Americans saw the continuing waves of white settlers as a threat not just to individual tribes, but to the whole Native American way of life.

Chapter Three

Andrew Jackson and the Indian Removal Act

"Established in the midst of a superior race, they must disappear."

—Andrew Jackson

The early years of the United States were a time of rapid change and political turmoil. At the beginning of the 1800s, the single most powerful political group was the Federalist Party, also known as the Pro-Administration Party. The Federalist Party was generally conservative in outlook, supporting banks, business, and manufacturing, opposing the French Revolution, and favoring trade with Britain ahead of other European countries.

Then, in the late 1790s, a new political party was created by two of the original Founding Fathers: Thomas Jefferson and James Madison. The Democratic-Republican Party opposed the Federalist Party by supporting state rights over federal control. In 1801, Thomas Jefferson became the first Democratic-Republican president, remaining in office for eight years. He was followed by the other founder of the Democratic-Republican Party, James Madison, who served as president of the United States until 1817.

By the time of the presidential election in 1824, the once-powerful Federalist Party was in such disarray that it was not able to field a single credible candidate. All the candidates in that election were put forward by the Democratic-Republican Party, and the eventual winner was John Quincy Adams. Next, in the election of 1828, Andrew Jackson became the first president of the newly established Democratic Party. Jackson, a former general, had been involved in combat in the War of 1812 and had led a brutal campaign against the Seminole people in present-day Florida in 1818.

Previous presidents, including Thomas Jefferson, had espoused a policy of peaceful integration and, where appropriate, relocation for Native American people and particularly for the Five Civilized Tribes—the Chickasaw, Choctaw, Muscogee-Creek, Seminole, and Cherokee. These Native Americans were referred to as civilized because it was thought that they were able to live in harmony with white settlers. They were to be encouraged to integrate into U.S. culture and society through conversion to Christianity and by recognition of things such as the right to own property. This policy broadly followed the lead of George Washington, who had supported the right of Native American people to live in homelands east of the Mississippi provided that they did not attack white settlers. When Andrew Jackson took the position of president, however, it was immediately clear that he intended to pursue a much more aggressive and confrontational policy.

Almost as soon as he was inaugurated, Jackson waged war against the Cherokee people with such savagery (he recommended, amongst other things, that Cherokee women and children should be killed as part of policy of extermination) that he was given the nickname "Indian Killer" in the U.S. administration. His policy proved popular with the American people, and he was re-elected to serve a second term as president in 1832.

Jackson was opposed to the policy of previous administrations of dealing with Native American people as if they were foreign nations. As far as Jackson was concerned, these were Americans who were subject to the same laws and customs as all other American citizens. He was only prepared to consider any form of self-rule for Native American people if they agreed to relocate to federally mandated lands west of the Mississippi River. Jackson saw the removal of Native American people as an inevitable part of progress itself. If they insisted on remaining in their ancestral homelands, Jackson foresaw that the result would be annihilation for many tribes. Only if they agreed to relocate to reservations controlled by the federal government could they be assured of survival.

To make sure that the removal of Native Americans would proceed as he wanted, President Jackson began to press for new legislation, specifically the Indian Removal Act. This act would pave the way for legal enforcement of the mass relocation of large numbers of Native American people to new lands, far from their homelands. It would also give the lands which formerly belonged to these tribes to the control of the southern states. This was especially important in Georgia, the largest state at the time, where there was a bitter and continuing dispute between white settlers and the Cherokee people about ownership of large tracts of the state. If the Indian Removal Act was to be passed, it would mean that the Cherokee would be forced to move from their lands in Georgia.

There is good reason to believe that Jackson thought this was a merciful procedure which would safeguard tribes from certain annihilation. Jackson believed that if, for example, the Cherokee were not prepared to move from Georgia, they would simply be wiped out by settlers. It is also clear that he regarded the removal of Native American people from their ancestral homelands as part of an inevitable process. He told Congress that "philanthropy could not wish to see this continent restored to the condition in which it was found by our forefathers. What good man would prefer a country covered with forests and ranged by a few thousand savages to our extensive Republic, studded with cities, towns, and prosperous farms, embellished with all the improvements which art can devise or industry execute, occupied by more than 12,000,000 happy people, and filled with all the blessings of liberty, civilization, and religion?"

Not everyone supported the new act. Some people, including frontiersman Davy Crockett who was by this time a congressman for the state of Tennessee, spoke out against the act, as did many committed Christians, and there was bitter and extended debate in Congress. Despite this, on April 24, 1830, the U.S. Senate passed the Indian Removal Act by a vote of 28 to 19. On May 26, the House of Representatives passed the act by a vote of 101 to 97. Two days later, it was signed into law by President Jackson.

Within less than six months, the first relocation of Native American people would begin.

Chapter Four

Choctaw Removal in 1831

"My friends, circumstances render it impossible that you can flourish in the midst of a civilized community."

—Andrew Jackson

In 1824, a new division of the U.S. Department of War was formed. The Bureau of Indian Affairs (BIA) was a replacement for the previous Office of Indian Trade, which had been responsible for issuing licenses and regulating trade with Native American tribes. The new bureau was responsible for both trade and for the assimilation of Native American people into the United States, but it would also be directly involved in the relocation of Native American people.

The intended destination to which these people would be moved was Indian Territory (also known as Indian Country and the Indian Zone), lands west of the Mississippi River comprising much of the present-day states of Oklahoma, Kansas, Nebraska, and Iowa. The intention, which had been generally articulated without becoming a formal part of U.S. government policy since the administration of President Thomas Jefferson, was that Native American tribes would be relocated from lands east of the Mississippi to Indian Territory, and these lands would then be available to white settlers.

The first Native Americans to come to the attention of the BIA were the Choctaw people, a confederation of tribes located in east-central Mississippi and west-central Alabama. Up to the late 1700s, there was a flourishing trade between the Choctaw people and white settlers. The Choctaw provided fur, mainly in the form of deerskin, and in exchange they received goods including firearms and cloth made from wool. However, by the early years of the nineteenth century, deer were becoming scarce on lands to the east of the Mississippi River, and the Choctaw were increasingly forced to hunt to the west of the river, bringing them into conflict with the Osage and Caddo tribes.

Although there was not one formal chief of all the Choctaw people, one man represented large numbers of the eastern division of the tribe, Mushulatubbee. This chief wanted to maintain the flow of manufactured goods traded to the Choctaw, but as deer skins became scarce, he began to look at alternative ways of generating trade. Under the leadership of Mushulatubbee, the Choctaw began to raise and sell livestock and horses, produce some manufactured goods such as baskets, grow cotton, and even own slaves who were used to work on plantations. The supply of manufactured goods was important to chiefs, who used the distribution of these items to reward their followers and ensure loyalty.

From 1820 onwards, the Choctaw even welcomed Christian missionaries from whom they learned English as well as business-related skills such as arithmetic and new and more efficient methods of farming. In 1820, Mushulatubbee signed the Treaty of Doak's Stand, which gave the Choctaw land west of the Mississippi River, in present-day Arkansas, in exchange for the cession of land in Mississippi and Alabama to the U.S. government. Signing this treaty provided Mushulatubbee with gifts of manufactured goods, which he was able to redistribute to his followers. In the event, almost no Choctaw people took up the offer of land west of the river, and anyway, most of the land ceded under the treaty was quickly and illegally occupied by white settlers.

In 1824, the same land west of the Mississippi River was ceded back to the U.S. government in exchange for more payments. Chief Mushulatubbee let it be known that he would support further cession of land in Mississippi and Alabama if, in exchange, the U.S. government were to recognize him as the formal chief of all the Choctaw people.

In September 1830, Mushulatubbee was one of the signatories to the Treaty of Dancing Rabbit Creek in which the Choctaw people agreed to hand over around 11 million acres of land in present-day Mississippi in exchange for approximately 15 million acres of land in the Indian Territory in present-day Oklahoma. When the Indian Removal Act was signed into law in 1830, it made perfect sense to use the removal of the Choctaw people to their new lands as the prototype to test the theories of the relocation of Native American people. President Jackson was anxious that this first relocation should proceed as smoothly as possible in order to act as a model for other similar plans.

The Treaty of Dancing Rabbit Creek was formally ratified by the U.S. Senate on February 24, 1831, and the first relocation began in the late autumn of that year. The intention was to complete the relocation in three separate waves, each involving around one-third of the Choctaw people in three successive years. Many Choctaw were not happy with the relocation, and there were accusations that senior members of the tribe had been bribed to secure their agreement. However, once the treaty was signed, most seemed to accept that the move was inevitable. One Choctaw chief said in late 1831 that "our doom is sealed. There is no other course for us but to turn our faces to our new homes toward the setting sun."

The U.S. Secretary of War, John Eaton, assigned responsibility for the first wave of relocations to George S. Gains, an agent who had been working with the Choctaw for some time. In late 1831, around 7,000 Choctaw people left for Indian Territory. They were first taken by steamboat up the Arkansas and Ouachita Rivers. Then they were dropped to walk for the remainder of the journey—a distance of several hundred miles.

The winter of 1831/1832 was one of the worst ever experienced with extreme cold, almost constant heavy snow, floods, and ice-covered rivers. The BIA had failed to purchase sufficient provisions, winter clothing, and snow shoes, and the Choctaw suffered in the sub-zero conditions. No-one is certain how many Choctaw people died on the trip, but it is estimated that only around 5,500 of the 7,000 people who left Mississippi actually arrived in Indian Territory. One Choctaw chief named Little Rock was interviewed for the *Arkansas Gazette* and described the journey as a "trail of tears and death."

Finally, the Choctaw arrived in present-day Oklahoma (the word "Oklahoma" is of Choctaw origin and means "red people"). These first arrivals settled in Boggy Depot in the western part of Indian Territory, Doaksville in the southeast, and Skullyville in the northeast. By the time they arrived, it was too late to plant many crops, and as a result, more Choctaw died of starvation during 1832. Despite this and the deaths on the journey, the U.S. government seemed to feel that this first relocation of Native Americans had gone well and pressed ahead with plans for the second wave of emigration. However, there were concerns that the cost of the first wave had been excessive—the overall cost was twice what had been budgeted by the BIA. As a result, George S. Gains was dismissed, and responsibility for the second and third waves was passed to the U.S. Army.

Around 6,000 to 7,000 Choctaw agreed to join the second wave late in 1832, but in order to economize, the army reduced provisions and provided only five small wagons for every 1,000 people. This meant that virtually everyone, including the young, the elderly, and the infirm, had to walk on the long last leg of the journey. Captain William Armstrong, one of the U.S. Army assigned to assist in the move noted, "Fortunately, they are a people that will walk to the last, or I do not know how we could go on." Once again bad weather, including bitter winds and extreme cold, affected the Choctaw, and this was made worse by an epidemic of cholera which killed many.

In late 1833, the last wave of Choctaw relocation took place; this time the weather was less severe, and those who set out suffered fewer hardships. Only around 900 Choctaw joined this final relocation. By the spring of 1834, about 11,500 Choctaw were settled in Indian Territory.

Having heard of the privations of the journey, around 6,000 Choctaw refused to move to Indian Territory and remained in Mississippi. These people became the victims of increasing harassment and intimidation. One of the chiefs of the Choctaw who remained in Mississippi wrote in 1848 that "we have had our habitations torn down and burned, our fences destroyed, cattle turned into our fields and we ourselves have been scourged, manacled, fettered and otherwise personally abused, until by such treatment some of our best men have died."

Attempts to relocate the Choctaw continued throughout the nineteenth century, and as late as 1903, 300 Choctaw from Mississippi were persuaded to relocate to Indian Territory.

Chapter Five

Seminole Removal in 1832

"How smooth must be the language of the whites, when they can make right look like wrong, and wrong like right."

—Black Hawk

The Seminole people lived in Florida, which had only become part of the United States in 1819. In 1823, the Treaty of Camp Moultrie provided the Seminole with a reservation in the heart of Florida, below Tampa Bay. This region was too sandy and marshy for successful agriculture and lacked game to hunt. As a result and combined with severe droughts, the Seminole were afflicted by starvation and disease. For many, an opportunity to move to Indian Territory seemed to offer a welcome release.

In May 1832, the Treaty of Payne's Landing was signed. Under this treaty, the Seminole agreed to give up the lands they had been allocated in Florida and to move to Indian Territory. A clause of the treaty allowed a small party of Seminole chiefs to travel to Indian Territory to examine the lands they had been allocated there. When they arrived in late 1832, they were horrified to discover that they were to be placed within lands already occupied by their bitter enemies, the Creek people. Nevertheless, the chiefs were pressured into signing a statement, in which the Seminole people agreed to relocate to the new land.

Having heard where they were to be sent, many Seminole refused to relocate, and a bitter argument developed between the people of the various Seminole tribes. This continued until 1835 when the leader of a pro-removal group of Seminole was murdered. Over 400 of his followers then agreed to become the first Seminole people to move to Indian Territory. This group was first taken to New Orleans and then embarked on steamers, which would take them up the Mississippi and Arkansas Rivers before starting the overland journey to Fort Gibson in Indian Territory. They left New Orleans on April 23, 1836, arriving in Fort Gibson on May 23. Heavy rains and disease meant that only 320 of the 407 people who set off survived the journey.

The majority of Seminole people refused to leave Florida for lands controlled by the Creek. In late 1835, fighting broke out between the Seminole and the U.S. Army when a band of Seminole warriors attacked two companies of troops. Almost all of the 110 U.S. soldiers involved were killed in what became known as the Dade massacre. This sparked the Second Seminole War, which would last until 1842 and would become one of the most costly and deadly of all the Indian Wars.

During the course of the war, around 1,600 U.S. troops would lose their lives, and more than twice that number of Seminole people would die. The cost of prosecuting this war has been estimated at somewhere in the region of 30 million dollars. Seminole prisoners taken during the conflict were routinely shipped off to their new lands in Indian Territory but, as on the first relocation, many died en route. By the time that the Second Seminole War ended, only around 4,000 Seminole people had been relocated to Indian

Territory while an equal number remained in Florida, refusing to move.

The authorities in Florida continued to pressure the federal government to ensure that all Seminole relocate. The Seminole who remained in Florida retreated to remote areas and sought to limit their exposure to white people, but there were continuing minor clashes. U.S. troops were sent to the area to prevent further problems, but in December 1855, the situation in Florida exploded into open conflict once again when a band of Seminole warriors attacked a US Army camp and killed a number of soldiers. The conflict that followed would last for three years and would become known as the Third Seminole War.

In an attempt to persuade more Seminole people to move to Indian Territory, the U.S. government established a new Seminole reservation in Indian Territory, which was completely separate from the Creek Nation. As a further incentive, $500 was offered to each warrior willing to relocate and $100 to each woman. As a result, many Seminole agreed to relocate, and by May 1858, the Third Seminole War was officially declared to be over.

While the bulk of the Seminole people were by this time in their new reservation in Indian Territory, small numbers remained in Florida where they lived quietly, avoiding contact with white people. Even into the twentieth century, small numbers of Seminole continued to live in relative isolation in the Lake Okeechobee and Everglades regions of Florida.

Chapter Six

Creek Removal in 1834

"One does not sell the land people walk on."

—Crazy Horse

At one time, the Creek Nation was the most powerful confederation of Native American people in the southeast United States, occupying millions of acres of land in present-day Georgia, Alabama, and Florida. However, in February 1825, Creek chief William McIntosh, a man of mixed parentage who had a Scottish father, signed the Treaty of Indian Springs which agreed to hand over all Creek land in Georgia and some in Alabama to the federal government. McIntosh, also known as and was also known as Tustunnuggee Hutkee ("White Warrior"), and his followers were paid $200,000 and given land in Indian Territory.

Most Creek were wholly opposed to this treaty and noted that it had concluded without the approval of the Creek National Council, an act that was punishable by death under Creek law. As a direct result, McIntosh was killed in May of 1825 at one of the plantations he owned on the Chattahoochee River. In January 1826, a delegation of Creek leaders traveled to Washington, and the U.S. government agreed to nullify the Treaty of Indian Springs, the only time that a ratified treaty with Native American people was ever overturned.

In its place, the Creek leaders signed the Treaty of Washington, which returned Creek land within Alabama but allowed the state of Georgia to keep land ceded under the previous treaty. The first relocation of Creek people took place in 1827 when around 700 Creek who had supported William McIntosh moved to Indian Territory. Over the next few years, other small numbers of Creek moved to Indian Territory, culminating in a move of over 1,000 people in 1834. Most of these early emigrants were either supporters of William McIntosh or Creek who had previously occupied land ceded to Georgia under the Treaty of Washington.

In 1832, a delegation of Creek leaders traveled to Washington to negotiate yet another treaty which they hoped would secure the future of the Creek people in their homelands. The outcome was the Treaty of Cusseta, in which the Creek agreed to relinquish their sovereign claim to their land in exchange for being given legal title to that land. Under the terms of the treaty, each Creek chief was assigned a parcel of 640 acres and each Creek family a parcel of 320 acres. In theory, the Creek were then free to do what they wished with this land—either to sell it or to live on it for as long as they wanted. In actuality, things did not work out as planned.

White settlers illegally moved into Creek lands, destroying their hunting ground by clearing land and building farms. The U.S. government refused to intervene, and these incidents led to a number of minor confrontations before it escalated into full-scale war in 1836 when a Creek war party attacked the town of Roanoke in Georgia and killed most of the defenders. Creek warriors also began attacking farms, killing white settlers, and disrupting transport. President Jackson used this conflict, known as the Second Creek War, as an excuse to force the removal of all Creek people from their homelands along the Chattahoochee and Flint Rivers in present-day Alabama.

Jackson sent fourteen companies of U.S. Army troops to Georgia supported by more than four-hundred Marines and five Navy armed steamboats, which sailed up the Chattahoochee River. By mid-1837, the U.S. military forces had defeated the largest Creek warbands, though sporadic fighting continued for several years. Almost as soon as the fighting was over, the U.S. Army began rounding up the Creek for relocation to Indian Territory. This included small numbers of Creek tribes who had actually fought on the side of the U.S. government during the war.

Around 15,000 Creek men, women, and children were assembled at Fort Mitchell, close to the Chattahoochee River. From there, the Creek were driven over 750 miles to Fort Gibson in Indian Territory. Unlike the previous Choctaw and Seminole relocations, there was no attempt to assist the defeated people who set out on this mammoth three-month journey. No wagons were provided, and the Creek took with them only what they could carry. They faced harsh weather, disease, and starvation on the way, and by the time that they finally arrived, more than 3,500 of them were dead.

For the survivors, survival was just as difficult in their new home. Each person was issued with a blanket by the U.S. Army and then essentially abandoned to their fate. In 1832, there were thought to be around 22,000 Creek living in Alabama and Georgia. By the time that the forced relocation was completed in the summer of 1837, all remaining Creek were living in Indian Territory, and there were only around 12,000 of them were left.

Chapter Seven

Chickasaw Removal in 1837

"We never had a thought of exchanging our land for any other . . . fearing the consequences may be similar to transplanting an old tree, which would wither and die away."

—Levi Colbert

In the presidential election of 1836, Andrew Jackson decided not to run, and the most prominent candidate was his former vice-president, Martin Van Buren. Unlike Jackson, Van Buren had no military background and no history of being involved in conflicts with Native American people. Van Buren won the election fairly easily, but it quickly became apparent that a new president would not bring a change in official policy towards Native American people.

In his first address to Congress in early 1837, Martin Van Buren said of the Native Americans in the southeast, "If they be removed, they can be protected from those associations and evil practices which exert so pernicious and destructive an influence over their destinies." With breathtaking hypocrisy, Van Buren seemed to be saying that the forced removal of these people was not just necessary, but it was for their own good, conveniently ignoring the thousands who had died on the long journey to Indian Territory.

Yet the fate of Native American people was not the first priority for the new president. Just a few weeks after Van Buren took office, America was afflicted by a major financial crisis, the Panic of 1837, which led to a depression that lasted until the early 1840s. For most of his time in office, finding ways of dealing with the economic crisis became the main focus for Van Buren, and the relocation of Native American people became much less important.

The Chickasaw people had already been the focus of several previous treaties which reduced their lands when they became the next target for federal scrutiny in 1837. By that time, these people who had once ruled over a large area were confined to the heart of their homelands, in northwestern Alabama and northern Mississippi. Unlike many other tribes, the Chickasaw had adapted relatively well to their new lands. Traditional hunting was difficult, and many Chickasaw people had become successful farmers operating prosperous small farms and plantations. Just like the other Native American people in this area, however, the Chickasaw were under pressure from the illegal encroachment on their lands by white settlers and from the U.S. government which wanted them to be removed to Indian Territory.

The situation became more serious when, in 1830, the state legislature of Alabama and Mississippi passed new statutes which made following tribal law a crime punishable by hefty fines. Between 1833 and 1837, Chickasaw leaders traveled to Washington to negotiate a treaty under which the tribe might be prepared to relocate to Indian Territory. Once a suitable area on which the Chickasaw could settle had been agreed, the Treaty of Doaksville was signed under which the Chickasaw agreed to relocate.

In 1835, the tribe began selling their lands in Mississippi and Alabama. Unlike the Creek and Seminole, the Chickasaw were not involved in armed conflict with the U.S. Government and so were allowed more time to realize profits from the sale of their homelands and were allowed to use these to pay for the costs of relocation to Indian Territory. In total, the Chickasaw raised more than three million dollars from the sale of land. In 1837, the first relocation began. The journey was still long and arduous, but the Chickasaw were better provided with provisions, wagons, and horses, which made progress easier. In November 1837, one astonished observer near Memphis watched as the great caravan passed, "Those going by land have been crossing the river for several days—a great many Chickasaw have fine wagons and four or five thousand horses."

By early 1838, the majority of the 4,000 Chickasaw had reached Indian Territory, though small groups continued to arrive for many years after. The last Chickasaw did not leave their homelands in Mississippi and Alabama until 1850. Compared to the tribulations of the Creek, Seminole, and Choctaw, the relocation of the Chickasaw people was relatively orderly and, because the tribe paid for it themselves, better provisioned and equipped. However, there were still deaths on the journey, and once the Chickasaw were settled in Indian Territory, life was not easy.

Warbands of Kickapoo and Shawnee warriors had established camps in the Washita Valley, in the heart of Chickasaw land in Indian Territory, and on its western edge there were hostile Comanche and Kiowa. Violence between the Chickasaw and these new neighbors was frequent as were outbreaks of disease and hunger caused when crops failed due to drought. The dislocation from their homelands also brought changes to Chickasaw culture and society. One of the issues was that the land on which the Chickasaw settled in Indian Territory was actually under the control of the much larger Choctaw tribe. Although the Chickasaw shared history and cultural links with the Choctaw, they were a distinct and different people. It wasn't until 1856 that the Chickasaw were finally able to completely separate themselves from the Choctaw and form their own tribal government.

Compared to the privations and deaths suffered by the Creek, Choctaw, and Seminole, the relocation of the Chickasaw may seem relatively benign, but it mustn't be forgotten that this was a move forced on these people, and in addition to hardships it led to irreversible changes in their society, culture, and way of life. There would be nothing benign about the relocation of the last of the Five Civilized Tribes which was to follow.

Chapter Eight
Cherokee Removal in 1838

"Long time we travel on way to new land. People feel bad when they leave old nation. Women cry and make sad wails. Children cry and make men cry, and all look sad like when friends die, but they say nothing and just put heads down and keep go towards West."

—Cherokee survivor of the Trail of Tears

The Cherokee were one of the largest and most powerful tribes in the southeastern United States, controlling lands in present-day Georgia, North Carolina, Tennessee, and Alabama. In 1802, the U.S. government made an agreement with the state of Georgia that, in return for the cession of the state's unincorporated western lands (which would later become Alabama and Mississippi), all Indian lands within Georgia would become the property of the state. That included the majority of the Cherokee homelands.

To encourage the Cherokee to move, in 1815 a reservation was created in the Arkansas district of the Missouri Territory. This reservation stretched from north of the Arkansas River to the southern bank of the White River. Small numbers of Cherokee people agreed to move to this new reservation and these people became known as the "Old Settlers," but the majority of the tribe refused to move and remained in their lands in Georgia.

New treaties were signed in 1817 and 1819 in which the Cherokee agreed to exchange their lands in Georgia for new land west of the Mississippi River in the Arkansas Territory. Again, small numbers of Cherokee people moved to the new lands, but the majority remained in Georgia. In 1820, the Cherokee people founded the Cherokee Nation modeled on the U.S. Constitution with elected officials, a Senate, and a House of Representatives. One of the first laws passed by the new Cherokee legislature made the sale of Cherokee lands a crime punishable by death. In 1825, the Cherokee National Council established its capital in what is now the city of Calhoun in Georgia, and in 1827, a formal, written constitution was drafted which declared the Cherokee Nation to be a sovereign and independent nation.

Then, in 1828, gold was discovered in White County in Georgia. This was within the boundary of the land claimed by the Cherokee Nation, and this discovery intensified calls to have all Native Americans removed from the area. In 1830, the state of Georgia attempted to have state laws extended to cover Cherokee lands. The Cherokee objected, and the Cherokee National Council sent delegates to challenge this in the Supreme Court in Washington. In 1831, the court rejected the Cherokee appeal and stated that the Cherokee Nation was not a sovereign and independent nation. This, combined with the passage of the Indian Removal Act in 1830, opened the way for the federal government to forcibly remove the Cherokee from their lands in Georgia.

The Jackson administration began to apply pressure to the Cherokee to sign a treaty of removal, but this was refused. When Jackson was reelected in 1832, some

Cherokee began to believe that relocation was inevitable and that it was better to accept this and to try to negotiate the best possible terms rather than resist. The Cherokee Nation became divided into pro and anti-relocation factions, and a bitter internal struggle began. The state government in Georgia, meanwhile, became so certain that the Cherokee would be removed that it organized a lottery to divide the Cherokee lands amongst white settlers.

In 1836, a treaty was signed between members of the pro-relocation faction within the Cherokee Nation and the U.S. government. This faction was led by a Cherokee leader called Kah-nung-da-tla-geh ("man who walks on mountaintop"), popularly known as Major Ridge, who was supported by his sons John Ridge and Buck Oolwatie. Ridge was a personal friend of President Andrew Jackson and had commanded a unit of Cherokee volunteers that fought on the side of the U.S. Army in the Creek War of 1813. As a result of this, Ridge was awarded the title of major, which he used for the rest of his life. Ridge did not command large-scale support within the Cherokee Nation, and a majority saw his signature of the treaty as a betrayal.

The Treaty of New Echota agreed to pay a large indemnity to the Cherokee people in return for their agreement to move to Indian Territory. This treaty was not signed by a single elected member of the Cherokee National Council, and there is good evidence that it was not supported by the vast majority of Cherokee people. Despite this, Congress ratified the treaty in May 1836 and agreed a deadline of May 1838 for the complete removal of the Cherokee people from Georgia. By 1838, Andrew Jackson was no longer president, but his successor, Martin Van

Buren told Congress that "a mixed occupancy of the same territory by the white and red man is incompatible with the safety or happiness of either." It was clear that the federal government was determined to enforce the Treaty of New Echota even though this was of dubious legality.

In May 1838, President Van Buren sent a force of 7,000 U.S. troops to Georgia under the command of General Winfield Scott. Their orders were to remove the Cherokee to Indian Territory, using whatever force was necessary. They were supported by the Georgia Guard, a militia with a reputation for extreme brutality. In the course of just three weeks, Scott's men rounded up or killed every Cherokee in North Georgia, Tennessee, and Alabama. Whole families were removed from their homes, sometimes at gunpoint, and placed in overcrowded holding camps built specially to hold the Cherokee until they could be deported. One eyewitness reported that "the scenes of distress defy all description. In many instances they were dragged from their homes without change of clothing and marched one hundred and twenty or thirty miles through heat and dust and rain and mud, in many cases bare-footed."

Looters followed the troops, ransacking homesteads and stealing whatever they could as the Cherokee were removed. This brutal and arbitrary process allowed families no time to collect their possessions, and many arrived at the camps with nothing more than the clothes they wore. A lack of food and insanitary and rat-infested conditions which led to the spread of disease caused the deaths of large numbers of Cherokee in the holding camps while they awaited forced relocation.

Around 1,000 Cherokee were able to escape from the camps and fled to the mountains of North Carolina (where their descendants still live today). The remainder began the long journey to Indian Territory. Three relatively small groups of Cherokee were transported by riverboats from Chattanooga in present-day Tennessee to the mouth of Sallisaw Creek near Fort Coffee. Most Cherokee were not, however, transported by riverboat and instead were forced to undertake the 2,000-mile journey on overland trails.

Starting in August 1838, groups of 700-1,500 Cherokee people began their long, grim journeys to Indian Territory. The route they followed wound through Tennessee, southwestern Kentucky, and southern Illinois. It then crossed the Mississippi River and made its way through southern Missouri and northwest Arkansas before finally arriving in Indian Territory near the present-day city of Westville. Each group of Cherokee were guarded and forced onwards by detachments of U.S. troops. Conditions on the march swiftly became horrendous.

Illness, exhaustion due to the arduous journey and disease took a terrible toll of the Cherokee people. The federal government stated officially that there were around 400 deaths on the journey. But a missionary doctor, Elizur Butler, who had been involved in both the holding camps and the journey to Indian Territory, later claimed that over 2,000 Cherokee died in the camps and at least 2,000 more on the journey. Some estimates put the total number of dead as high as 8,000. Whatever the precise number, there is little doubt that the forced move from Georgia to Indian Territory killed very large numbers of Cherokee people. One U.S. soldier noted in his journal, "I fought in many wars between the states and have seen many men killed, some by my own hands, but the Cherokee Removal was the cruelest work I ever knew."

Another U.S. soldier wrote in his memoirs of these events, noting, "Murder is murder, and somebody must answer. Somebody must explain the streams of blood that flowed in the Indian country in the summer of 1838. Let the Historian of a future day tell the sad story with its sighs, its tears and dying groans. Let the great judge of all the earth weigh our actions and reward us according to our work."

Even when they finally arrived in Indian Territory, the survivors of the Trail of Tears faced new challenges. Many of the Old Settlers, Cherokee people who had moved to the territory some time before, were well established. The majority of these people were part of the pro-relocation faction and included Major Ridge, the Cherokee who had signed the Treaty of New Echota. There was immediate friction when large numbers of anti-relocation Cherokee arrived in the area.

Eventually the anti-relocation faction took control of the Cherokee Nation, and a new constitution was ratified. In a final act of retribution, the former leaders of the pro-relocation faction, Major Ridge and his sons John and Buck, were murdered in 1839.

The forced relocation of the Cherokee people was one of the most brutal of all the forced relocations of Native American people. Almost one-quarter of the total population of the Cherokee Nation died as a direct result of incarceration in holding camps and the journeys which followed. Incredibly, President Martin Van Buren told Congress that the Cherokee had "emigrated without any apparent reluctance." In his memoirs, he said of the relocation of the Cherokee that "We were perhaps in the beginning unjustifiable aggressors, but we have become the guardians and, as we hope, the benefactors." The Cherokee now refer to these events as *Nu na da ul tsun yi* ("the place where they cried").

Chapter Nine

Legacy

"We are now about to take our leave and kind farewell to our native land, the country that the Great Spirit gave our Fathers, we are on the eve of leaving that country that gave us birth . . . it is with sorrow we are forced by the white man to quit the scenes of our childhood . . . we bid farewell to it and all we hold dear."

—Charles Hicks

Few white Americans objected to the forced relocation of the Five Civilized Tribes of Native American people while they were happening. Partly this was because most reporting was done by white reporters and published in newspapers intended for a predominantly white readership. The U.S. government also sought to portray the relocations as necessary, inevitable, and generally successful, and this included dramatically under-reporting the numbers of deaths. The indifference of many people to these events was also the result of racial stereotyping. Native Americans were often portrayed as semi-nomadic migratory hunters who followed game wherever it was available. Such people, it was assumed, would have no particular attachment to a certain geographic area and would be able to live just as well in one place as another. This wasn't true, of course.

Many tribes had, under the influence of white settlers, become successful farmers, raised domesticated livestock, and most lived in settled villages and towns. Despite this, most white Americans still believed Native Americans to be savages—when Martin Van Buren was asked to explain why the war against the Seminole people was still raging near the end of his presidency, he blamed the "wily character of the savages." There is no evidence that this attitude was any different to the views held by the majority of Americans.

For the people forced to migrate to new lands, life was not easy. The landscape and terrain of Indian Territory itself was not too different to the lands they had left behind, but to the west lay the vast emptiness of the Great Plains, home of marauding bands of Kiowa, Comanche, Wichita, and Apache. Although Indian Territory theoretically extended all the way to the headwaters of the Arkansas, Red, and Canadian Rivers, the Great Plains and their hostile inhabitants presented a barrier which the relocated people could and would not cross.

The Native American people relocated to Indian Territory did adapt to their new environment—a missionary reported in 1840 that the Choctaw were settled in villages comprising log cabins, and they were growing crops of corn, pumpkins, peas, melons, and yams. This was achieved at the cost of abandoning many elements of their society and culture. The Five Civilized Tribes did not disappear after the Trail of Tears, but they were forced into new ways of life which often mirrored white society.

The forced relocations of these people were not the only forced relocations of Native American people nor was the Cherokee removal the last such event. For example, the passing of the Kansas-Nebraska Act in 1854 led to an influx of white settlers to this area, and the Native American people who lived there were put under pressure to leave.

The implementation of the Indian Removal Act and the forced removal of Native American people from the southeast of the United States was one of the causes of an event which no-one could foresee in the 1830s. The expulsion of Native Americans led to an explosion of white settlers to these areas and to the emergence of a new and lucrative cash crop: cotton. These new lands combined with the availability of slave labor became the mainstay of the economy of the southern states. By 1860, the annual production of cotton from these states had reached over three million bales weighing five-hundred pounds each. The reliance of the southern states on the cotton crop and the reliance of the cotton industry on slavery was one factor that led directly to the attempt by the South to secede from the Union, which caused the outbreak of the American Civil War in 1861.

After the war ended in 1865, there was another surge of settlers to the west which put pressure on Native American people. The Medicine Lodge Treaty signed in 1867 led to the move of southern Plains Indians to reservations in Indian Territory. One of the last reservations to be created in Indian Territory was set up to receive Geronimo's band of Chiricahua Apaches in 1894.

During the Reconstruction Era, the lands assigned to Native American people as reservations were substantially reduced. In March 1889, President Benjamin Harrison signed a proclamation opening Indian Territory to white settlers. Indian Territory itself formally ceased to exist in

1907 when the Oklahoma Enabling Act created the state of Oklahoma by combining Indian Territory and Oklahoma Territory.

The reservation system continued, and Indian reservations still exist across the United States. These are still controlled by the Bureau of Indian Affairs though the tribes on each reservation are regarded as sovereign and are not subject to federal laws. Still, life on these reservations is not easy. Most suffer from very high rates of infant mortality, alcohol and drug abuse, poverty, and unemployment.

Conclusion

Some modern historians and writers have used terms such as "ethnic cleansing" to describe the treatment of Native American people during what has become known as the Trail of Tears. This is deliberately emotive, but it is difficult to argue against.

The Five Civilized Tribes were so-called because they were the tribes most trusted to live in harmony with white settlers. Yet when their land became desirable for settlement, they were removed in a brutal and arbitrary manner, and thousands died as a direct result. That all this was done within the auspices of the law and with the approval of the U.S. government makes it even more difficult to justify.

Government approval is, in fact, one of the reasons why the forced relocations are now widely recognized as one of the most shameful episodes which occurred during the colonization of America by white settlers. It is unacceptable when individuals commit acts of violence and intolerance, but when these acts are directed, sanctioned, and approved by the president and all the apparatus of government, they become altogether more sinister.

The Trail of Tears and the other forced relocations which followed effectively destroyed the Native American culture and ways of life. Instead, these people were forced to adopt "modern" values and society, something to which many found they were ill-suited. The legacy of this can still be seen in the unduly low life expectancy that continues to affect the Native American population of the United States today.

Made in the USA
Middletown, DE
16 May 2025

75635367R00027